CHURCH PLANTING PRODUCES EVANGELISM AND DISCIPLESHIP

SESSION 6

DR. AARON R. JONES
Foreword by Dr. Timothy M. Hill

Interfacing Evangelism and Discipleship

WORKBOOK

Church Planting Produces Evangelism and Discipleship

Dr. Aaron R. Jones

Interfacing Evangelism and Discipleship – Church Planting Produces Evangelism and Discipleship

Copyright © 2018 by Dr. Aaron R. Jones

Printed in the United States of America

Published by Kingdom Publishing, LLC, Odenton, MD 21113

All rights reserved. No part of this book may be reproduced or transmitted in any form or by any means, electronic or mechanical, including photocopying, recording or by any information storage and retrieval system without written permission from the author, except for the inclusion of brief quotations in a review.

All scripture quotations are from the King James Version of the Bible. Thomas Nelson Publishers, Nashville: Thomas Nelson, Inc. 1972

Editor: Sharon D. Jones

Graphic Designer: Janell McIlwain – JM Virtual Concepts

                Tiara Smith

ISBN 978-1-947741-21-8

Table of Contents

Interfacing Evangelism and Discipleship **Sessions** 1

Foreword 2

Introduction 3

5 Statistics Every Church Planter Needs to Know 7

Myths of Church Planting 11

Basic Church Plant Components 15

Bi-Vocational Dynamic 20

Benefits of a 21

Bi-Vocational Pastor 21

G. R. A. C. E. 25

Developing the Team 29

The DNA-Acts 6:3 33

How to Mobilize the Team 36

Works Cited 39

About the Author

Contact Page

Interfacing Evangelism and Discipleship
Sessions

Session 1—**Introduction and Philosophy**

Session 2—**5 Principles to Encourage Evangelism**

Session 3—**Components of Evangelism**

Session 4—**Bait for Evangelism**

Session 5—**Methodology of Evangelism**

Session 6—**Church Planting Produces Evangelism and Discipleship**

Session 7—**Babes in Christ**

Session 8—**Components of Discipleship**

Session 9—**Evangelism and Discipleship Plan**

Session 10—**Spirit of Forgiveness**

Foreword

When God calls a man of faith and fortitude to a specific purpose in the building of His Kingdom, He uses an individual like Dr. Aaron Jones.

Feeling the urgency of the hour, Dr. Jones has shaped his participation in the FINISH Commitment by emphasizing the merging of evangelism and discipleship strategies to assist churches and individuals in their quests to effectively reach the lost. As Senior Pastor of New Hope Church of God, he is well-aware of what it takes to affect the Great Commission of our Lord.

Dr. Jones' desire is to instruct others on how to deliberately make an impact on winning souls and then discipling them for powerful Christian service. His all-inclusive approach will intrigue and provide the impetus for those willing to pursue the heart of God.

Interfacing Evangelism and Discipleship will change the course of your outreach!

Dr. Timothy M. Hill
General Overseer
Church of God, Cleveland, Tennessee

Introduction

Introduction

■ Each church has its own personality and is able to reach certain groups of people.

_____
_____
_____

■ It has been said that the survival of the Church in many ways is dependent on church planting.

_____
_____
_____

■ Paul was a great church planter, leader, and mentor.

_____
_____
_____

- Paul saw the need to plant churches as a way to spread the Gospel of Jesus Christ.

___

___

___

- Church plants has the opportunity to bring new energy, connections, and new vision to a community.

___

___

___

- Evangelism and Disciple must be the focus of all church plants.

___

___

___

- The single most effective evangelistic methodology under heaven is planting new churches," according to Peter Wagner (1990).

___

___

___

Introduction

■ Denominations and mission boards are investing much time, money, and personnel into church planting.

_____

_____

_____

■ Networks of churches, like Stadia, ARC, Acts 29 and New Thing Network and NAMB have come together for the primary purpose of planting new churches (Churchplanting.com)

_____

_____

_____

Additional Notes

5 Statistics Every Church Planter Needs to Know

Statistics[1]

1 Less than 18% of Americans attend church

_____
_____
_____

2 There are 156 million unchurched in the US.

_____
_____
_____

3 47% of America's unchurched is open to being invited to church by a friend.

_____
_____
_____

4 Churches that plant, grow three times faster.

_____
_____
_____

5 A new church gains 60-80% of its membership from new conversion.

_____

_____

_____

Additional Notes

Myths of Church Planting

Myths of Church Planting

❶ Myth #1: *Church planting will hinder the growth of other churches.*

_____
_____
_____

② Myth #2: *There are already enough churches in our community.*

_____
_____
_____

③ Myth #3: *Church planting is not a successful tool for growth in the body of Christ.*

_____
_____
_____

④ Myth #4: *Our church cannot support a church plant.*

_____
_____
_____

⑤ Myth #5: *Church planting creates division in the body of Christ.*

_____
_____
_____

❻ Myth #6: *Church planting makes existing churches irrelevant.*

_____
_____
_____

Additional Notes

Basic Church Plant Components

Basic Church Plant Components

- Know your calling

_____
_____
_____

- Know your community

- Conduct a Demographical Study

- Identify the Vision

- Identify the Purpose

- Know your Core Values

   _____
   _____
   _____

- Have an Outreach Plan

   _____
   _____
   _____

- Connect with partners/supporters/community leaders/local schools

   _____
   _____
   _____

- Recruit a Launch Team

   _____
   _____
   _____

- **Develop a Timeline**

  _____

  _____

  _____

- **Create a Budget**

  _____

  _____

  _____

Additional Notes

Bi-Vocational Dynamic

Bi-Vocational Dynamic

- It has been said that two-thirds of churches in America are pastored by bi-vocational pastors.

- Also, only 7% of pastors in Protestant churches are between the ages of 28–45.

Benefits of a Bi-Vocational Pastor

Benefits of a Bi-Vocational Pastor[2]

- There is usually a stronger financial base for both the pastor and the church.

___
___
___

- A stronger financial base allows the ministry to do more outreach and missions.

_____

_____

_____

- Pastors lead with more freedom because they are less afraid of obstinate leaders. Obstinate leaders don't threaten his/her complete livelihood.

_____

_____

_____

- They tend to engage more laypersons in ministry—out of necessity.

_____

_____

_____

- Congregation adjusts its expectations—they don't expect you to be superman or superwoman.

_____
_____
_____

- They may be more in touch with everyday challenges of a person who works and faces the trials of vocation.

_____
_____
_____

- They stay fresh in their ability to engage in personal evangelism (at work).

_____
_____
_____

- They tend to maximize time because they have to do more with less time.

_____
_____
_____

Additional Notes

G. R. A. C. E.

G. R. A. C. E.[3]

G.R.A.C.E. is an acrostic to encourage bi-vocational pastors and church planters.

- G—God
- R—Relationship
- A—Affirmation
- C—Care
- E—Expectation

- Always keep _____ as the focus—not ministry.

_____
_____
_____

- Intentionally cultivate your personal _____ with Christ.

_____
_____
_____

- Learn to affirm yourself and accept _____ from those closest to you.

_____
_____
_____

- You MUST practice _____.

_____
_____
_____

G. R. A. C. E.

- Adjust your _____.

_____

_____

_____

Additional Notes

Developing the Team

Developing the Team

Questions to Ask

- What is the make-up of a good team?

  _____

  _____

- What should be the DNA of a good team?

  _____

  _____

■ How do you mobilize your team (How do you help them become effective)?

_____
_____
_____

- Children's Leader

_____
_____
_____
_____

- Worship Leader

_____
_____
_____
_____

- First Impressions Leader

  _____

  _____

  _____

  _____

- Administrative Support/Leader

  _____

  _____

  _____

  _____

Additional Notes

The DNA-Acts 6:3

The DNA—Acts 6:3[4]

■   Integrity—Your team members must be people who demonstrate high integrity.

_____

_____

_____

- **Spiritual**—Your team members must be spiritual.

  _____
  _____
  _____

- **Competent**—Your team members must be competent.

  _____
  _____
  _____

- **Committed**—Your team members must be committed.

  _____
  _____
  _____

The DNA-Acts 6:3
Additional Notes

How to Mobilize the Team

How to Mobilize a Team

- Train Them

_____
_____
_____

- **Empower Them**

_____
_____
_____

- **Release Them**

_____
_____
_____

Additional Notes

Works Cited

[1]"6 Statistics Every Church Planter Needs to Know," Portable Church, 2016, www.portablechurch.com/2016/06/

[2]Izzard, James, GRACE for the Tentmaker-Manuscript. (Upper Marlboro, Maryland), 2017.

[3]Izzard, James, GRACE for the Tentmaker-Manuscript. (Upper Marlboro, Maryland), 2017.

[4]Izzard, James, GRACE for the Tentmaker-Manuscript. (Upper Marlboro, Maryland), 2017.

About the Author

DR. AARON R. JONES serves as Senior Pastor of New Hope Church of God. Under his pastorate is New Hope Kiddie Kollege, Inc (Daycare) and New Hope Community Outreach Services, Inc. Dr. Jones also oversees New Hope Church of God Ghana (2 churches) and New Hope Church of God Uganda (3 churches).

Dr. Jones is an Ordained Bishop with the Church of God denomination and is the DELMARVA-DC District Overseer (16 churches). Dr. Jones serves on DELMARVA-DC's Regional Council, Ministerial Internship Program Board, Urban Ministry Committee, Finance Committee, and Chaplain's Board. He also serves on both the Church of God's International and DELMARVA-DC Ministry to the Military Board. In his local community, Dr. Jones serves as a Chaplain for the Charles County Sheriff Department. He also serves as Board Secretary for the United Ministers Coalition of Southern Maryland, Inc.

Being obedient to 2 Timothy 2:15, "Study to show thyself approved…," Dr. Jones received a Doctorate in Theology and Pastoral Counseling from Life

Christian University and a Doctorate in Christian Counseling from American Christian College and Seminary. He is a certified Pastoral Counselor with the International Association of Christian Counseling Professionals. He is a Life and Pastoral Coach. He is the former Executive Vice President of the National Bible College and Seminary in Fort Washington, Maryland.

Dr. Jones has published ten books and a soul-wining project that provide a biblical foundation for Christian doctrine and discipline. He has recorded a CD entitled, Peace in the Storm. He is the founder and owner of God's Comfort Ministries, LLC, which provides Christian literature, evangelism training, and spiritual guidance. He has appeared live on TCT Network; WATC-TV's Atlanta Live; Babbie's House (hosted by CCM artist Babbie Mason); and In Concert Today on DCTV. He has done radio interviews with Radio One's WYCB's program; The Praise Fest Show; and online with Total Prayze. He was featured on the cover of Change Gospel Magazine and interviewed on Promoting Purpose Magazine.

Dr. Jones not only serves God, but his country as well. He has served over 20 years in the Armed Forces. He is a retired Chaplain with the Army National Guard. He participated in both Operation Noble Eagle (2003) and Operation Iraqi Freedom III (2005).

Dr. Jones is happily married to the former Sharon Russell. He sincerely believes without her love, support, and encouragement, many of his goals would not have been accomplished.

Contact Page

Mailing Address:

150 Post Office Road #1079

Waldorf, Maryland 20604

Website: www.godscomfort.net

Email: drjones@godscomfortmin.net

Facebook: God's Comfort Ministries

Twitter: @GodsComfort_Min

Instagram: @godscomfort_min

GOD'S COMFORT MINISTRIES

God's Comfort Ministries (GCM) provides practical Christian books, teachings, trainings, and coaching to new converts and seasoned believers. GCM provides understanding of the doctrinal principles of the Bible.

Services Provided

Pastoral and Life Coaching

Evangelism and Discipleship Training

Spiritual Guidance

New Author Consultation

Christian Literature

www.ingramcontent.com/pod-product-compliance
Lightning Source LLC
Chambersburg PA
CBHW081357080526
44588CB00016B/2522